Thirty-One Days of Prayer

FOR OTHERS

ALEXA HESS

PRAYERS FOR

Contents

If we are honest, many of us would admit that we do not pray as we should. Prayer can be difficult, and sometimes we do not know what to pray about or how to pray. Praying for ourselves is one thing, but praying for others is often more easily neglected.

The truth is that it can be easy to get wrapped up in our own world. We can develop tunnel vision, only thinking and praying about the things pertaining to ourselves. We can look back on the day and regretfully see that we did not pray for a single person.

In 1 Timothy 2:1, Paul writes, "I urge that petitions, prayers, intercessions, and thanksgivings be made for everyone." But do we really pray for all people? Maybe we pray for the people we live with or see the most. While it is a good thing to pray for these people, we often miss the opportunity to pray on behalf of all God's people.

It is a beautiful gift to intercede for others. Christ modeled praying for others in His High Priestly Prayer in John 17. On the night before His death, Jesus spent time praying fervently on behalf of those in His care and those who would come to believe in Him. This powerful intercession is what we have the privilege of entering into as brothers and sisters in Christ.

This booklet is designed to help you grow in praying for others by walking you through 31 days of prayer. Each day will have a category or person and a scripture to read and prompts to help guide your prayers. There will also be a daily action step to put into practice what you prayed for that day.

As you go throughout each day, ask that God will help these prayers become a regular part of your routine. The goal of the Christian life is not to have a perfect prayer life but a fruitful prayer life, full of prayers for everyone around you.

Pray that God would prepare your heart for the next 31 days of prayer. Ask that this booklet will help foster a deeper love for others and a habit of intercession. Pray that you will be focused each day and just as joyful to pray for one person or group of people as you are each of the others.

Dear Heavenly Father,

Prayers for a Heart for Others

WHAT KEEPS YOU FROM PRAYING FOR OTHERS?

WHAT DO YOU NEED TO DO TO PRAY FOR OTHERS MORE?

Read Philippians 2:3-4

Confess to the Lord any way that you do not pray for others as you should. Pray that God would rid you of any selfishness in your heart. Ask that you would count others as more significant than yourself, and pray that your mind would be full of the interest of others and not just your own.

Read James 2:1, 8-9 & 1 John 3:17

Pray that you will have a heart that seeks to pray for all people. Ask that there will be no partiality within you and that you will see it necessary to pray for every person. Pray that your heart will not be open to one person and closed to another.

Read Genesis 1:27 & John 13:34

Pray that God will remind you of the worth and value of other people. Ask that He will fill your heart with love toward others. Pray that He would remove any bitterness you may feel toward another, and ask that you would love that person as Christ does.

Besides using this book, take another practical step that helps you to remember to pray for others. Text a friend after you finish a day in this book, and ask how you can pray for him or her. Keep a journal of prayer requests for other people, or set a reminder on your phone to pray for a particular person.

WHAT WILL YOU BEGIN DOING TO PRAY FOR OTHERS MORE?

A Prayer for a Heart for Others

_____

_____

_____

_____

_____

_____

_____

_____

_____

_____

_____

_____

_____

_____

_____

_____

_____

_____

_____

_____

_____

_____

_____

_____

_____

_____

_____

Amen

DAY 2

Prayers of Gratitude for Others

TAKE A MOMENT TO WRITE DOWN THE PEOPLE IN
YOUR LIFE FOR WHOM YOU ARE GRATEFUL.

NOW, WRITE DOWN WHY YOU ARE THANKFUL FOR THEM.

Read Ecclesiastes 4:9-12 & Psalm 106:1 ✓

Thank God for the gift of friendship. Thank Him that He has blessed you with people to strengthen you and help you. Thank God for the specific qualities you listed about the people you are thankful for.

Read Philippians 1:3-4 & Ephesians 1:16

Thank God for the people He has placed in your life. Ask that you will remember them often, and pray for them continuously with a joyful heart. Pray that you will not take friendship for granted but will always have gratitude. ✓

Read 1 Thessalonians 1:2

Pray that other people will speak words of thanksgiving to these people. Ask that they would be surrounded by people who recognize their character, gifts, and hard work and praise them for it. ✓

Write a thank you card to a friend, or post a picture of your friend on social media saying why you are grateful for him or her.

WHAT WILL YOU DO THIS WEEK TO SHOW GRATITUDE
TOWARD ANOTHER?

A Prayer of Gratitude for Others

_____

_____

_____

_____

_____

_____

_____

_____

_____

_____

_____

_____

_____

_____

_____

_____

_____

_____

_____

_____

_____

_____

_____

Amen

DAY 3

Prayers for Friendships

WHO ARE THE FRIENDS IN YOUR LIFE?

IN WHAT WAYS DO YOU WANT TO GROW AS A FRIEND?

Read Proverbs 17:17

Pray that your friends would feel loved today. Ask that you would spur this on by being a friend who loves at all times. Pray that the Lord will remind them that they are special and cared for by the Lord and other people who are near. ✓

Read Hebrews 10:24-25 & Hebrews 3:13

Pray that your friends would feel encouraged today. Ask that the Lord will lift up their heads if they are feeling down. Pray that God would put people in their paths today who will speak words of love and kindness to them. ✓

Read Numbers 6:24-26

Pray this prayer over your friends: ✓

Lord bless _____, and keep them; make Your face shine on them, and be gracious to them. God, turn Your face toward them, and give them peace.

Look back on the ways you want to grow as a friend. List 1-3 practical steps that you can take to grow in these ways. For example, if you want to grow in your encouragement of others, you could gather uplifting scripture to send to a friend.

WHAT WILL YOU BEGIN DOING TO GROW IN YOUR FRIENDSHIP WITH OTHERS?

A Prayer for Friendships

_____

_____

_____

_____

_____

_____

_____

_____

_____

_____

_____

_____

_____

_____

_____

_____

_____

_____

_____

_____

_____

_____

_____

Amen

DAY 4

Prayers for Broken Relationships

WHAT BROKEN RELATIONSHIPS ARE PRESENT IN YOUR LIFE?

WHAT BROKEN RELATIONSHIPS DO YOU SEE AROUND YOU?

Read Ephesians 4:32 & Romans 12:14

Pray that you will have forgiveness toward the people who have hurt ✓
*you. Ask that you would not hold their offenses against them. Pray that
the Lord will bless them and that God will keep your heart free from ill
wishes toward them.*

Read 1 Peter 3:11 & Luke 17:3

Pray that people will have their eyes opened to how they are hurting
*others. Ask that they would seek forgiveness and stop the ways they are
causing pain or harm to others. Pray that you would have the boldness
to confront others about their sin toward you or another.*

Read 2 Corinthians 13:11

Pray that there will be reconciliation in the broken relationships you listed. Ask that their hearts will be softened toward one another and that they would seek to mend the relationships they have broken.

If you have a broken relationship with another person, take a step toward reconciliation. This could involve asking to meet to talk about what is hurting your relationship or asking for forgiveness.

WHAT WILL YOU DO THIS WEEK FOR A
BROKEN RELATIONSHIP?

A Prayer for Broken Relationships

Amen

Prayers for Those in Unrepentant Sin

HEART CHECK

Is there any unrepentant sin in your own heart that needs to be ✓
confessed? Before continuing in this day, pray for God to reveal
any places in your heart where there is unrepentant sin.

WHO DO YOU KNOW WHO IS IN UNREPENTANT SIN?

WHAT UNREPENTANT SIN DO YOU SEE AROUND YOU?

Read 2 Corinthians 7:9-10 & 1 John 1:9

Pray that the Holy Spirit would convict unrepentant sinners of their sin. Ask that they would not continue to indulge in this sin and would recognize their need to repent and turn away from their sin. Pray that they would not just regret their sin but be grieved by it so that it leads to repentance. Ask that their eyes will be opened to the truth that confession is met with God's forgiveness. Pray that they would take that step of repentance and confess their sin to God.

Read James 5:19-20 & Galatians 6:1-2

Pray that the Lord will use the people in unrepentant sinners' lives to help bring them to repentance. Ask that God will give people the words to speak truth to those in unrepentant sin and that they will listen. Pray that those who know an unrepentant sinner will be given endurance to continue pursuing the person, confronting him or her in boldness but also in a spirit of gentleness.

Read James 4:11-12

Pray that the Lord would keep your heart free from bitterness toward unrepentant sinners. Ask that your righteous anger over their sin would not turn into a sinful rage against them. Pray that your heart would be in the right place when you think of those in unrepentant sin and that you would always be led to pray for them instead of thinking or speaking ill of them.

It can be easy to become frustrated when a person we know remains in unrepentant sin. Instead of causing our frustrations to keep us from trying to help this person, keep making efforts to speak truth into this person's life. Remember not to do so in a spirit of anger or shaming your friend for the sin. Continue to remain present in this person's life, and use the relationship between the two of you to create a welcoming place to share.

WHAT WILL YOU DO THIS WEEK FOR SOMEONE IN
UNREPENTANT SIN?

A Prayer for Those in Unrepentant Sin

Amen

DAY 6

Prayers for Justice

HEART
CHECK

Look inward by assessing any areas in your life where you are contributing to injustice. Are there any stereotypes or prejudices you need to confess? Pray that the Lord would reveal any areas of injustice in your heart, and confess these to Him.

WHAT INJUSTICE DO YOU SEE IN THE WORLD?

Read Psalm 10:12-15 & Psalm 34:17-18 ✓

Pray that God will vindicate those who are being oppressed or wrongly accused. Ask that God would bring comfort to those who are being mistreated. Pray that the oppressed would be delivered from their bondage and be brought to safety.

Read Romans 12:19

Pray that people will not retaliate against injustice in sinful ways. Ask that they would not seek vengeance but would be peaceable in their opposition to injustice. Pray that they would place vengeance in the hands of God who will punish all evil acts. ✓

Read 1 Peter 3:9-11

Pray that God would move in the hearts of those who are acting unjustly. Ask that the oppressors would see the error of their ways and would repent. Pray that people would work together to expose injustice instead of contributing to it.

An important step in engaging with justice is to educate yourself on what injustice is occurring in the world so that you can recognize it and speak out against it. Spend some time this week reading articles or picking up a book that speaks to what is happening in the world.

WHAT WILL YOU COMMIT TO THIS WEEK IN ENGAGING AGAINST INJUSTICE?

A Prayer for Justice

Amen

Prayers for Peace

HEART CHECK

Ask the Lord to reveal areas of your heart where you are not being a ✓
peacemaker, and confess to Him. Examine your heart to identify any
anger. Consider if you have been unkind to someone, or assess whether
your actions are contributing to strife.

WHO ARE THE PEOPLE IN YOUR LIFE WHO NEED PEACE?

WHAT PEOPLE IN THE WORLD NEED PEACE?

Read 2 Thessalonians 3:16 & John 14:27

Pray for the peace for those who are troubled. Ask that they be reminded
of the peace of God and rest in His peace. Pray that they would trust ✓
in Him, knowing that as the Prince of Peace, He will bring about
healing and restoration.

Read Matthew 5:9

Pray for those who are contributing to unrest in the world. Ask that they would see that their actions are causing pain and suffering and be moved to repentance. Pray that people would abandon anger or selfish actions in order to be peacemakers instead.

Read 1 Timothy 2:1-4

Pray that those in governmental and leadership positions would be proponents of peace. Ask that they would not illicit strife. Pray that leaders would demonstrate godly actions that lead to peace for those they govern.

When we look at the need for peace from a global standpoint, we can feel as if our actions do not play a part. But even the smallest of actions can begin chain reactions of peace among people. Think of one or two ways you can promote peace in your community. For example, attend a city meeting to learn more about what is happening in your city and what projects you can join in to promote peace and unity. Or pledge to say something kind to a stranger each day this week.

ACTION STEP

WHAT WILL YOU DO THIS WEEK TO LIVE OUT AND PROMOTE PEACE?

A Prayer for Peace

_____

_____

_____

_____

_____

_____

_____

_____

_____

_____

_____

_____

_____

_____

_____

_____

_____

_____

_____

_____

_____

_____

_____

Amen

DAY 8

Prayers for the Grieving

WHO ARE THE PEOPLE IN YOUR LIFE WHO ARE GRIEVING?

WHAT PEOPLE IN THE WORLD ARE GRIEVING?

Read Psalm 34:18 & Matthew 5:4

Pray that they will be reminded that God is near to the brokenhearted. Ask that they will feel the presence of God comforting them. Pray that they would draw near to God during this time and not pull away from Him.

✓

PRAYER PROMPTS

31

Read Romans 12:15

Pray that the Lord will surround your grieving friends with others who will mourn alongside them. Ask that God will give people wisdom for how to comfort and the right words to speak. Pray that those who are grieving will not pull away from people but be vulnerable with them.

Let any of your friends who are grieving know that you are thinking of and praying for them by sending a card, bringing a meal, or meeting a tangible need.

WHAT WILL YOU DO THIS WEEK FOR SOMEONE WHO IS GRIEVING?

A Prayer for the Grieving

_____

_____

_____

_____

_____

_____

_____

_____

_____

_____

_____

_____

_____

_____

_____

_____

_____

_____

_____

_____

_____

_____

_____

_____

_____

Amen

Prayers for the Suffering

WHO ARE THE PEOPLE IN YOUR LIFE WHO ARE
EXPERIENCING SUFFERING?

WHAT PEOPLE IN THE WORLD ARE EXPERIENCING SUFFERING?

Read 2 Corinthians 4:16-18

*Pray that those who are suffering would not lose heart. Ask that they ✓
will rest in the truth that through the power and strength of Christ,
they are being renewed. Pray that the future glory awaiting them is
larger in their eyes than the affliction they are experiencing. Ask that
they will hope in what they cannot see, knowing that there is
eternal purpose, even in their pain.*

Read Romans 8:17-18 & Romans 5:3-5

*Pray that they will not give up but have endurance through their
suffering. Ask that they would see how God is using their suffering
to grow them closer to Christ and more like Christ. Pray they will
boast in their suffering, knowing that it produces endurance,
character, and hope.*

Read 2 Corinthians 1:3-4 & Galatians 6:2

Pray that they will be surrounded by others who will help to carry their burdens. Ask that they will feel the comfort that comes from Christ through the comfort of others. Pray that they would be honest with others about their suffering so that others can come alongside them and provide help and support.

Depending on the type of suffering, it may seem difficult to know how to enter into the suffering alongside them. Often, the best way to help those who are suffering is to sit with them and listen to how they are feeling. Go to any you know who are suffering, and ask to be with them. Offer to listen to what they are experiencing, or simply keep them company.

HOW WILL YOU HELP SOMEONE WHO IS SUFFERING THIS WEEK?

A Prayer for the Suffering

_____

_____

_____

_____

_____

_____

_____

_____

_____

_____

_____

_____

_____

_____

_____

_____

_____

_____

_____

_____

_____

_____

_____

_____

Amen

Prayers for the Lonely

WHO ARE THE PEOPLE IN YOUR LIFE WHO ARE LONELY?

Read Psalm 27:7-10

Pray that those who are lonely will seek the Lord, including those who ✓ are not believers. Ask that they would rest in the help that comes from the Lord. Pray that they would find comfort in knowing that the Lord will never reject but always receive His own.

Read Romans 8:35-39 & Deuteronomy 31:6

Pray that in their loneliness, the Lord will remind them that His love is always with them. Ask that they will rest in the truth that if they are in Christ, they are never separated from God's love. Pray that they will find comfort in the presence of God that never leaves them.

Read 1 Thessalonians 5:11

Pray that God will bring people to surround them this week with reminders that they are not alone. Ask that He will give them community that encourages and uplifts them. Pray that their loneliness will be combated by the presence and care of others.

If you know any who are lonely, do not wait for someone to go to them. Invite them to join you for a meal or coffee, or offer to come to them if they cannot leave the house. If you cannot physically go to them, call them, and remind them how much you care for them. Remind them that they may feel alone but that they are never alone.

WHAT WILL YOU DO FOR SOMEONE THIS WEEK
WHO IS LONELY?

A Prayer for the Lonely

_____

_____

_____

_____

_____

_____

_____

_____

_____

_____

_____

_____

_____

_____

_____

_____

_____

_____

_____

_____

_____

_____

_____

_____

_____

Amen

DAY II

Prayers for the Depressed

WHO ARE THE PEOPLE IN YOUR LIFE WHO ARE DEPRESSED?

Read Psalm 40:1-2

Pray that those who are depressed will see God as the one who delivers ✓
them. Ask that they will cry out to the Lord, knowing He hears them
and turns toward them. Pray they will rest in the strength of God, who
provides them with a firm foundation on which to stand.

Psalm 42:5-11

Pray that in their depression, they will remember who the Lord is. Ask
that they will put their hope in God. Pray that they will pray honest
prayers like David. Ask that they will rest in God's love and praise
Him, even in their pain.

Psalm 23

Pray that they will find comfort in the security of the Good Shepherd.
Ask that they will rest in the protection and care that comes from Him.
Pray that they will see Him as the one who renews them in their
darkness and leads them through their darkness.

Similar to helping someone who is suffering, make yourself available to sit with those who are depressed. Give them the space to shed tears. If you cannot go to a person, put together a playlist of worship songs to send that will speak truth.

WHAT WILL YOU DO FOR SOMEONE THIS WEEK WHO IS DEPRESSED?

A Prayer for the Depressed

Amen

DAY 12

Prayers for the Anxious

WHO ARE THE PEOPLE IN YOUR LIFE WHO ARE ANXIOUS?

Read Isaiah 26:3

Pray that they will keep their minds fixed on Christ. Ask that their ✓
minds will not stay on their anxieties but on Jesus. Pray that they will
rest in God's perfect peace, trusting in Him.

Read 1 Peter 5:7

Pray that they will cast all of their anxieties on Christ. Ask that they
would not withhold any of their anxieties but give them all to Him.
Pray that they will do so knowing that Jesus cares for them always,
especially in their fears.

Read Philippians 4:6-7 & Psalm 34:4

Pray that they will ask the Lord to deliver them from anxiety. Ask that
they will be strengthened through prayers of petition and thanksgiving
to Him. Pray that they will see God as the one who guards their hearts
and minds against anxious thoughts. Ask that they would rest in His
peace that surpasses all understanding.

Anxiety looks different for every person, and there is no one solution for all anxiety. Even though anxiety can be varied and layered, a helpful way to bring about relaxation for someone with anxiety is to put together a small gift basket with items that might help to soothe and calm them.

WHAT WILL YOU DO FOR SOMEONE THIS WEEK WHO IS ANXIOUS?

A Prayer for the Anxious

_____

_____

_____

_____

_____

_____

_____

_____

_____

_____

_____

_____

_____

_____

_____

_____

_____

_____

_____

_____

_____

_____

_____

_____

_____

Amen

DAY 13

Prayers for the Sick

WHO ARE THE PEOPLE IN YOUR LIFE WHO ARE SICK?

IN WHAT WAYS DO THEY NEED HEALING?

Read Psalm 103:1-5

Pray the Lord's healing over those who are sick. Ask that as the great ✓
physician, He will touch them and bring about healing. Pray that
they will praise the One who delivers and restores.

Read 2 Corinthians 1:3 & Psalm 55:22

Pray that they will feel the Lord's comfort in their sickness. Ask that
in their pain and suffering, they would draw close to the Lord.
Pray that they would ask the Lord for His help and rest in His
power that sustains them.

Read Isaiah 40:29 & Romans 15:13

Pray that they will have strength and endurance in sickness. Ask that they will rely on the strength of the Lord when they feel weak. Pray that instead of feeling hopeless, God would renew their hope and give them perseverance.

Organize a group of your friends to each film a video of encouragement for your friend who is sick. Have them share how they are praying and include encouraging words and verses. Be sure to include your own video, piece them all together, then send the video to your friend.

HOW WILL YOU ENCOURAGE A FRIEND WHO IS
SICK THIS WEEK?

A Prayer for the Sick

_____

_____

_____

_____

_____

_____

_____

_____

_____

_____

_____

_____

_____

_____

_____

_____

_____

_____

_____

_____

_____

_____

_____

_____

_____

_____

Amen

DAY 14

Prayers for the Weary

WHO IN YOUR LIFE DO YOU KNOW IS WEARY?

IN WHAT WAYS ARE THEY WEARY?

Read Matthew 11:28-30

Pray that those you know who are burdened would stop trying to carry
*their burdens on their own and would instead lay them down at Jesus's
feet. Ask that they would find their rest in Jesus. Pray that they find
comfort in the peace that comes from Christ's rest.*

Read Isaiah 40:29-31

*Pray that they would renew their strength in the Lord. Ask that they
trust in Him and see Him as their place of refuge. Pray that they
find endurance in the Lord and rest in the power He gives them to
keep moving forward.*

Read Colossians 1:9-11 & Ephesians 3:14-19

Pray that they would be strengthened with all power according to His glorious might, with endurance, patience, and joy. Ask that they be strengthened with power through the Spirit. Pray that they would be rooted and grounded in the great love Christ has for them.

You may not be able to remove someone's burden but you can do something that helps lighten the load. For a worn-out mother, this could be watching her child so she can rest. For a friend overwhelmed at work, this could look like providing a meal.

WHAT WILL YOU DO FOR SOMEONE THIS WEEK
WHO IS WEARY?

A Prayer for the Weary

_____

_____

_____

_____

_____

_____

_____

_____

_____

_____

_____

_____

_____

_____

_____

_____

_____

_____

_____

_____

_____

_____

_____

_____

Amen

Prayers for the Doubting

WHO DO YOU KNOW WHO DOUBTS THEIR FAITH?

Read Mark 9:23-24 & Luke 17:5

Pray that they ask for the Lord's help in their doubts. Ask that their doubting would not lead them away from Christ but would motivate them to cling more closely to Him. Pray that the Lord will increase their faith and that His truth would be louder than the doubts.

Read Colossians 2:6-8

Pray that the Lord would remove things from their lives that are contributing to their doubt. Ask that they would be grounded in the truth of the gospel and not swept away by false doctrine or deceptive philosophy. Pray that they would take their questions to God's Word and other believers instead of looking to misguided sources.

Read 1 John 2:1-6

Pray that they would have assurance in their faith. Ask that they would not see their doubts to mean they do not belong to Christ. Pray that they would see evidence of their salvation by their love for Jesus and how they are walking with Him.

Make yourself available for any who are doubting. Invite them to ask you questions they are struggling with, and open God's Word together to help answer them. Consider going through a book together that aids in tackling specific doubts.

WHAT WILL YOU DO THIS WEEK FOR SOMEONE
WHO IS DOUBTING?

A Prayer for the Doubting

_____

_____

_____

_____

_____

_____

_____

_____

_____

_____

_____

_____

_____

_____

_____

_____

_____

_____

_____

_____

_____

_____

_____

_____

Amen

DAY 16

Prayers for Unbelievers

Read Acts 3:19 & John 17:3 ✓

Pray that they would come to know Jesus Christ and believe in the one true God. Ask that they would have an understanding of the gravity of sin and be led to repentance. Pray that they would recognize their need for Christ.

Read Romans 10:9-10, 14-15

Pray that the Lord would bring others to share the gospel with these people. Ask that the Holy Spirit would move through these conversations to bring about salvation. Pray that they would call on the name of the Lord, declare Jesus as Lord, and truly believe the gospel.

Read 2 Corinthians 4:3-5

*Pray that the Holy Spirit would remove the veil from their eyes.
Ask that the Holy Spirit would open their eyes to see the light of
the gospel and believe it. Pray that the enemy would not
have his hold on them any longer.*

Sometimes with unbelievers, we can become discouraged that they are not coming to know Christ. Do not let this stop you from persevering in sharing the gospel with them. Come up with one way that you can share the gospel with someone this week.

HOW WILL YOU SHARE THE GOSPEL WITH AN
UNBELIEVER THIS WEEK?

A Prayer for Unbelievers

_____

_____

_____

_____

_____

_____

_____

_____

_____

_____

_____

_____

_____

_____

_____

_____

_____

_____

_____

_____

_____

_____

_____

Amen

DAY 17

Prayers for Neighbors

WHO ARE YOUR NEIGHBORS?

Read Galatians 6:10 & Matthew 7:12

Pray for interactions this week with other neighbors that will be encouraging to them. Ask that those in the neighborhood would be kind and hospitable to them. Pray that they would have joy in the area where they live, knowing they have people around them who care for them.

Read Psalm 121:7-8

Pray that the Lord will protect them. Ask that no harm will come to their homes. Pray that God will keep them and their families safe.

Read Matthew 5:16

Pray for any unbelieving neighbors to come to know the Lord. Ask that in your interactions with them, you would be a gospel witness. Pray that God will stir in their hearts a desire to know Him and that He will open their eyes to the gospel.

Invite a neighbor to join you and your family for dinner or a game night. If you are not familiar with your neighbors yet, bake some cookies for them, and introduce yourself!

ACTION STEP

WHAT WILL YOU DO THIS WEEK FOR YOUR NEIGHBORS?

A Prayer for Your Neighbors

_____

_____

_____

_____

_____

_____

_____

_____

_____

_____

_____

_____

_____

_____

_____

_____

_____

_____

_____

_____

_____

_____

_____

_____

Amen

Prayers for Missionaries

WHO ARE THE MISSIONARIES YOU KNOW?

Read Psalm 121:8

Pray that the Lord will protect them in the places they are serving. ✓
Ask that He will keep them safe from any persecution. Pray that they
can continue to spread the gospel with no harm coming to them.

Read Colossians 4:3-4

Pray that the Lord will move in the hearts of the people these
missionaries work with to believe the gospel. Ask that God would
provide them opportunities to share the gospel with them. Pray that
God would give them boldness to speak the good news of the gospel.

Read Galatians 6:9 & Philippians 4:19

Pray that God would give them endurance when their work is hard or seems unfruitful. Ask that the Lord would give them perseverance and trust that He is using them where they are located for a reason. Pray that the Lord would provide for them and that they will not fear but trust that He will take care of them.

Spend some time researching where missionaries are serving. Pick two or three missionaries/locations, and dedicate daily prayer time to praying for these people and places.

WHAT WILL YOU DO THIS WEEK FOR MISSIONARIES?

A Prayer for Missionaries

_____
_____
_____
_____
_____
_____
_____
_____
_____
_____
_____
_____
_____
_____
_____
_____
_____
_____
_____
_____
_____

Amen

Prayers for the Poor

WHERE IS THERE POVERTY AROUND YOU?

WHERE IS THERE POVERTY IN THE WORLD?

Read Psalm 140:12 & Proverbs 29:7

Pray that the Lord will bring about justice for those in poverty. Ask ✔
that God will make a way to bring them out of poverty. Pray that
others will not disregard the poor but seek justice for them.

Read Proverbs 14:21, 31

Pray that those who are poor will receive kindness from others. Ask that
no one will look down on them but will be kind and compassionate
toward them. Pray that no one will treat them cruelly or unfairly.

Read 1 John 3:17-18

*Pray that people will serve the poor and make provisions for them.
Ask that people, including yourself, will have hearts open to those
in poverty. Pray that the poor will see the love of Christ through
the kind actions of others.*

Sometimes we may feel helpless in resolving poverty, but the smallest actions can make a difference. Research shelters in your area, and volunteer to serve. Work with your church to collect donations, or put together bags of necessities to give to the poor.

WHAT WILL YOU DO THIS WEEK FOR THE POOR?

A Prayer for the Poor

_____

_____

_____

_____

_____

_____

_____

_____

_____

_____

_____

_____

_____

_____

_____

_____

_____

_____

_____

_____

_____

_____

_____

_____

_____

Amen

Prayers for the Church

IN WHAT WAYS DO YOU WANT TO GROW AS
A CHURCH MEMBER?

Read 1 Corinthians 1:10 & 2 Timothy 2:22-24

Pray that the Church will remain in harmony and be kept from division. Ask that the body of Christ would refrain from selfish ambition and work together instead of against each other. Pray that any brokenness in the Church would be mended.

Read Philippians 2:4-6 & 1 Peter 2:9

Pray that the Church's actions will set itself apart from the world. Ask that it will be a light for the gospel and shine like stars against the darkness. Pray that the Church will not hinder the gospel witness but have integrity in the declaration of the gospel.

Read 2 Timothy 2:14-18

Pray that the Church will be grounded in the truth of God's Word. Ask that it will not shift due to the theology of today's world. Pray that the body of Christ will not be deceived by false doctrine and that the Church would remove any false teaching from the body.

Look back on the ways you want to grow as a church member. List 1-3 practical steps that you can take to grow in these ways. Choose one of these things to implement starting this week. For example, if you are not currently serving in your local church, choose an area to serve.

WHAT WILL YOU DO THIS WEEK FOR THE CHURCH?

A Prayer for the Church

_____

_____

_____

_____

_____

_____

_____

_____

_____

_____

_____

_____

_____

_____

_____

_____

_____

_____

_____

_____

_____

_____

_____

_____

Amen

Prayers for Church Leadership

WHO ARE CHURCH LEADERS IN YOUR LIFE WHO NEED PRAYER?

WHO ARE CHURCH LEADERS IN THE WORLD WHO NEED PRAYER?

Read 1 Peter 5:1-3

Pray that the leadership would shepherd the church body rightly. Ask that their hearts would be full of compassion and care for the church and that God would keep them from working selfishly or begrudgingly. Pray that they would set a good example for Christlikeness in their local churches.

Read 1 Timothy 3:1-10 & Titus 1:6-9

Pray that God would raise up leaders who embody these characteristics.
Ask that those who are currently in leadership would maintain these
qualities. Pray that the Lord would expose and remove leaders who are
disregarding these qualifications and leading from sinful hearts.

Read Titus 1:10-11 & 2 Timothy 4:2-5

Pray that leaders will remain dedicated to preaching sound doctrine.
Ask that they would be grounded in God's Word and will not shift
their theology to please the congregation. Pray that they will be bold to
stay true to God's Word and encourage the church body in truth.

Many church leaders do much for the local church with little to no recognition. Write a letter to your pastor or church leaders, thanking them for the work they are doing and how thankful you are for their leadership.

WHAT WILL YOU DO THIS WEEK FOR THOSE IN
CHURCH LEADERSHIP?

A Prayer for Church Leadership

Amen

DAY 22

Prayers for the Government

HEART
CHECK

Sometimes we may have bitterness in our hearts toward the government. We may disagree with leaders and laws, but we must maintain gentleness and respect, even as we call for justice and moral uprightness. Ask the Lord to reveal any areas of your heart that are bitter toward the government, and confess that bitterness to Him.

WHO ARE THE GOVERNING OFFICIALS IN YOUR CITY, STATE, AND COUNTRY?

Read 1 Peter 2:13-17

Pray that government leaders will seek to act justly and honorably. ✓ *Ask that God will give wisdom to leaders about making the right decisions and laws. Pray that their actions are for the good of the people and not their own gain.*

Read Isaiah 10:1-2 & Proverbs 22:8, 22-23

Pray that God would bring to justice those who are under oppressive leaders. Ask that God would remove those who are leading unjustly and replace them with leaders who will act rightly. Pray that God would remove unjust systems in the government and appoint leaders who will create just systems.

Read Romans 13:1-7

Pray that people will submit to the government. Ask that they will see the authority placed over them as authority that comes from God. Pray that they do not rebel against the government but seek to engage in it wisely and honorably.

Being an informed citizen helps us to know what is going on in the country. If we are not aware of what is happening in our city, state, and country, we can become blind to the ways we should respond ethically as Christians. Spend some time this week researching and reading about current events to educate yourself on what is occurring in the government and how to respond to it.

ACTION STEP

WHAT WILL YOU DO THIS WEEK AS A CITIZEN?

A Prayer for the Government

Amen

Prayers for the Employed

WHO ARE PEOPLE YOU KNOW WHO ARE EMPLOYED?

Read Colossians 3:17 & Colossians 3:23-24

Pray that their work will be for the glory of God and not man.
Ask that they will not do their work with any motives of selfish
gain or prideful acknowledgment. Pray they will work with
joyful and thankful hearts.

Read 1 Peter 3:15

Pray that they would be gospel witnesses in their workplace. Ask that
through their conversations with co-workers, they will be examples of
Christlikeness. Pray that they will have opportunities to share
the gospel with their co-workers.

Read Proverbs 14:23

Pray for endurance in their work. Ask that they will be kept from laziness and stay motivated in their jobs. Pray for God's strength to carry them through their days and for His help if they grow wearisome.

ACTION STEP

Buy The Daily Grace Co.'s "Encouragement for the Workplace" verse card set, and gift it to a working friend. If you are unable to buy them, create your own! Put together some encouraging notes and verses, and give them to a working friend, or leave them on a co-worker's desk.

WHAT WILL YOU DO THIS WEEK FOR A WORKER?

A Prayer for the Employed

Amen

Prayers for the Unemployed

WHO ARE THE PEOPLE YOU KNOW WHO ARE UNEMPLOYED?

Read Romans 8:28 & Deuteronomy 15:7-8 ✓

Pray that God will provide them with jobs. Ask that God would bring about job opportunities this week. Pray that the Lord would use the people in their lives to help them financially.

Read Philippians 4:19 & Matthew 6:25-34

Pray that they would trust the Lord to provide for them. Ask that when they begin to worry about their finances, they will rest in God's provision. Pray that the Lord would provide for their needs.

Read Psalm 71:14 & Psalm 9:18

Pray that they would not be discouraged while they await jobs.
Ask that they would remain hopeful that the Lord will give them jobs.
Pray that they will not feel defeated but will continue to endure in
finding jobs without giving up.

Do something practical this week that brings financial help to an unemployed person. Surprise that person by filling up his or her car with gas or providing groceries for the week.

WHAT WILL YOU DO THIS WEEK FOR SOMEONE UNEMPLOYED?

A Prayer for the Unemployed

_____

_____

_____

_____

_____

_____

_____

_____

_____

_____

_____

_____

_____

_____

_____

_____

_____

_____

_____

_____

Amen

DAY 25

Prayers for Parents

WHO ARE THE PARENTS IN YOUR LIFE?

PRAYER PROMPTS

Read Colossians 3:12-13

Pray that they will raise their children in a way that honors the Lord. ✓
*Ask that God will give them patience with their children and will
speak to them with kindness. Pray that they will be an example to their
children of the love of Christ by their words and attitude.*

Read Deuteronomy 6:6-7 & Ephesians 6:4

*Pray that they will raise their children through the instruction of God's
Word. Ask that they will exemplify Christlike character in the way
they discipline and teach their children. Pray that their homes would
be filled with the truth of the gospel.*

Read Psalm 18:1-2 & 1 Corinthians 15:58

Pray that God will give them endurance when parenting is hard.
Ask that God will give them strength when they are tired. Pray that
God will give them opportunities to rest.

Reach out to a parent in your life, and ask how you can care for him or her this week. Offer to do something that will lessen that parent's load, and follow through with that help. For example, help take care of the children when that parent is at work, or provide a meal for the family one night.

WHAT WILL YOU DO FOR A PARENT THIS WEEK?

A Prayer for Parents

_____

_____

_____

_____

_____

_____

_____

_____

_____

_____

_____

_____

_____

_____

_____

_____

_____

_____

_____

_____

_____

_____

Amen

Prayers for Children

WHO ARE THE CHILDREN IN YOUR LIFE?

Read Deuteronomy 6:6-7 & Proverbs 22:6

Pray that the children you know will listen to the biblical teaching of their parents. Ask that they will grow in their knowledge of the Lord and understanding of the gospel. Pray that they would come to saving faith in Christ.

Read Proverbs 4:1-2 & Ephesians 6:1-3

Pray that they will not be disrespectful but will honor their parents. Ask that they will be obedient to them and will listen to their instruction. Pray that they will see discipline as for their good.

Read James 1:19-20 & Proverbs 16:24

Pray that they would be kind to their parents and siblings. Ask that they will learn to control their tongues and speak edifying words. Pray that they would be slow to speak and slow to anger.

Buy a Daily Grace kids' book or another children's book, ask a friend with a child if you can babysit, and read the book to his or her child!

WHAT WILL YOU DO FOR A CHILD THIS WEEK?

A Prayer for Children

Amen

Prayers for the Childless

WHO IN YOUR LIFE IS CHILDLESS OR STRUGGLING
WITH INFERTILITY?

Read Psalm 61:1-5

Pray that those who are childless or struggling with infertility will √
be comforted by the Lord. Ask that they would bring their pain and
hurting to the Lord who hears their cries. Pray that they will have
community around them who will bring comfort in the pain.

Read Romans 12:12 & Psalm 27:14

Pray that God would bless them with children. Ask that He would
make a way for them to have a child. Pray that they would hope in
the Lord and continue to be persistent in prayer.

Read Proverbs 12:18 & Job 42:2

Pray that those around them will speak kind and careful words to
them. Ask that they would not feel shame for being childless. Pray that
they would not view themselves as incomplete without a child but be
reminded of the purpose God has for them.

Give a gift to someone who is struggling with infertility as a way to encourage them and let them know you care. Consider jewelry designed specifically to encourage women who are walking through infertility. Prayer plants can also be a thoughtful gift to remind someone that you are praying for them.

WHAT WILL YOU DO THIS WEEK FOR SOMEONE WHO IS CHILDLESS?

A Prayer for the Childless

Amen

Prayers for Marriages

WHO ARE THE MARRIED PEOPLE IN YOUR LIFE?

Read Ephesians 5:22-28

Pray that the marriages of those you know would be a reflection of ✓
Christ and the Church. Ask that the wives would reflect the way the
Church submits to Christ by submitting to their husbands. Pray that
the husbands would reflect the sacrificial love of Christ by the way they
love and care for their wives. Ask that Christ would remain the center
of these marriages as they submit to one another.

Read Proverbs 15:1 & James 3:17

Pray that they would encourage and build up each other. Ask that they
would be kind and gentle in speech and attitude. Pray that they would
refrain from anger and seek to resolve conflict calmly.

Read Romans 12:9-10 & 1 Peter 4:8

Pray that they would look for opportunities to serve each other.
Ask that they would refrain from selfishness but live sacrificially.
Pray they would not take advantage of the care of their spouses
but seek to show the same levels of love and service.

Buy a gift card to use at a restaurant, and give it to a married couple so that they can have a date night! If they have kids, take an extra step by watching their kids while they are at dinner.

WHAT WILL YOU DO FOR A MARRIED COUPLE THIS WEEK?

ACTION STEP

A Prayer for Marriages

Amen

Prayers for Singles

WHO ARE THE SINGLE PEOPLE IN YOUR LIFE?

Read Philippians 4:11-13 & Galatians 2:20

Pray that they would not feel incomplete without a spouse. ✓
Ask that they will find contentment in their relationships with the Lord. Pray that their identities would be found in the Lord and not in a relationship status.

Read Ephesians 4:31 & Isaiah 49:13

Pray that God would comfort them when they feel lonely or discouraged in their singleness. Ask that they would not have bitterness toward those who are married or in relationships. Pray that others would not overlook them but include them in plans and spend time with them.

Read Psalm 138:8 & Matthew 28:16-20

Pray that they would not feel without purpose in not having a spouse. Ask that God would show them opportunities in their lives to serve Him and others. Pray that they would take hold of the calling to be disciple-makers and find joy in that calling.

ACTION STEP

Think of a practical way you can make a single person feel seen and cared for this week. For example, invite that person to lunch or a cup of coffee. Text that person to share that you are thinking of him or her, and ask how you can pray for that person.

WHAT WILL YOU DO FOR A SINGLE PERSON THIS WEEK?

A Prayer for Singles

Amen

Prayers for Widowed

WHO DO YOU KNOW IN YOUR LIFE WHO IS WIDOWED?

Read Psalm 68:5 & Psalm 147:2

Pray that the Lord would comfort them in the loss of a spouse. ✓
Ask that they would rest in the Lord when grief washes over them.
Pray that they would not grieve without hope.

Read 1 Timothy 5:3, 16

*Pray that God would bring others to take care of them. Ask that
they would feel cared for and supported by others. Pray that they will
ultimately rest in the provision that comes from God.*

If they feel comfortable, ask them to come over and share treasured memories, or look through old photos together.

WHAT WILL YOU DO THIS WEEK FOR A WIDOW?

A Prayer for Widows

Amen

Prayers for Loved Ones

WHO ARE YOUR LOVED ONES?

Read Psalm 121:7-8

Pray that God will protect your loved ones. Ask that the Lord would keep them safe this week. Pray that He would watch over them and keep them from harm.

Read Romans 5:6-11

Pray for any family members who are not believers to come to know the Lord. Ask that God would give you and other believing family members opportunities to share the gospel with them. Pray that the Holy Spirit would open their eyes to the truth of the gospel.

Read 1 Timothy 5:1-2, 8

Pray that you will stay present in the lives of your loved ones. Ask that you do not get so consumed with your immediate family that you forget to think of and care for your loved ones. Pray that God will show you opportunities to care for them.

Think of your loved ones you have not spoken to in a while. Call them, and tell them how much you miss and love them.

WHAT WILL YOU DO FOR YOUR LOVED ONES THIS WEEK?

A Prayer for Loved Ones

Amen

How have you seen God work in your prayer life?

Thank you for studying
God's Word with us!

CONNECT WITH US
@thedailygraceco
@kristinschmucker

CONTACT US
info@thedailygraceco.com

SHARE
#thedailygraceco
#lampandlight

VISIT US ONLINE
www.thedailygraceco.com

MORE DAILY GRACE
The Daily Grace App
Daily Grace Podcast